POP PERFORMANCE PIECES

Flute & Piano

ALL OF ME JOHN LEGEND 2

BRIDGE OVER TROUBLED WATER SIMON & GARFUNKEL 8

CLOCKS COLDPLAY 16

DON'T STOP BELIEVIN' JOURNEY 22

FIREWORK KATY PERRY 29

MAD WORLD MICHAEL ANDREWS FEAT. GARY JULES 34

A THOUSAND MILES VANESSA CARLTON 42

A THOUSAND YEARS CHRISTINA PERRI 37

WHEN WE WERE YOUNG ADELE 52

YOUR SONG ELTON JOHN 48

Published by
Chester Music

Exclusive Distributors:
Hal Leonard
7777 West Bluemound Road,
Milwaukee, WI 53213
Email: info@halleonard.com

Hal Leonard Europe Limited
42 Wigmore Street, Marylebone,
London WIU 2 RY
Email:
info@halleonardeurope.com

Hal Leonard Australia Pty. Ltd.
4 Lentara Court, Cheltenham,
Victoria 9132, Australia
Email: info@halleonard.com.au

Order No. CH85074
ISBN 978-1-78558-335-3

Flute consultant: Howard McGill.
Piano consultant: Lisa Cox.
Compiled and edited by Naomi Cook.
Music formatted by Sarah Lofthouse, SEL Music Art Ltd.

Photographs courtesy of Ruth Keating,
assisted by Lisa Cox and James Welland.
Special thanks to the pupils at St Benedict's
School, Ealing and their Director of Music
Christopher Eastwood for taking part in the photo
shoot.

Printed in the EU.

www.halleonard.com
www.wisemusicclassical.com

CHESTER MUSIC
part of The Wise Music Group

ALL OF ME

Words & Music by John Legend & Tobias Gad

Hints & Tips: Make sure you use the dynamics to help build interest in the piece, being careful not to overpower the melody. There are many held notes throughout — resist the urge to rely on the pedal to sustain the notes rather than holding them for their full value. Practise without the pedal first!

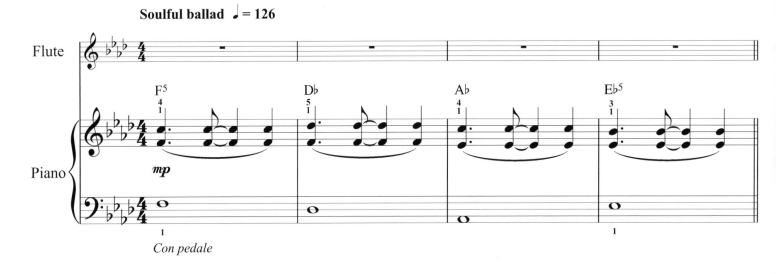

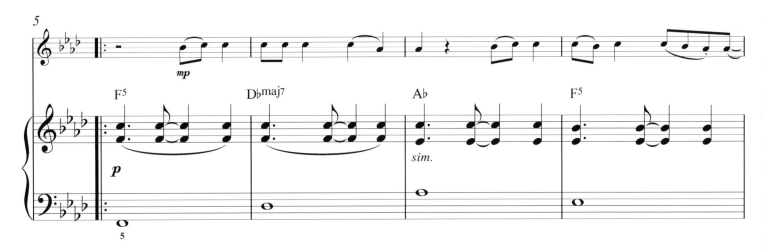

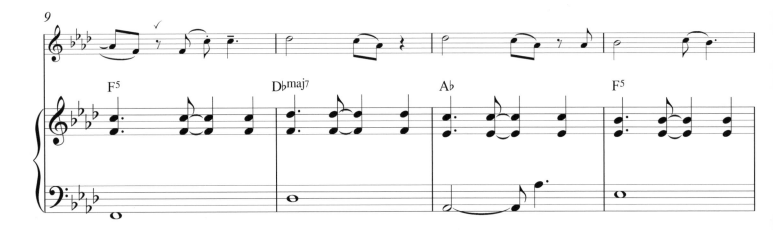

3

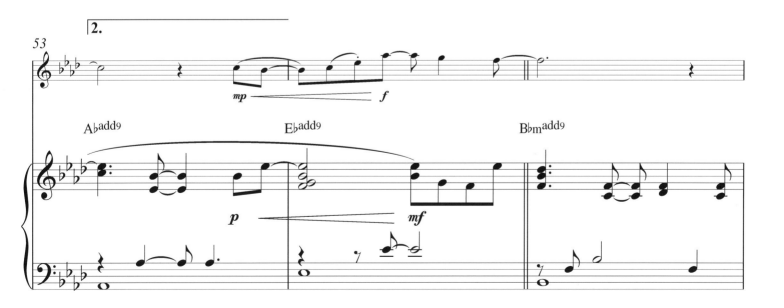

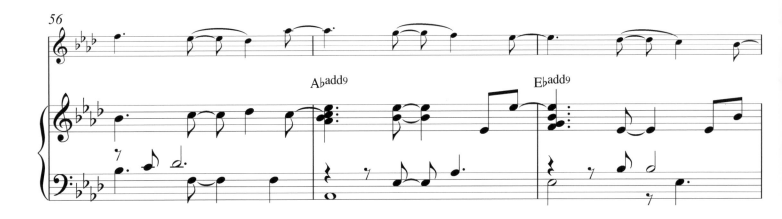

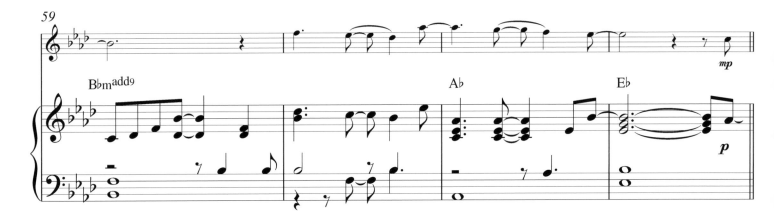

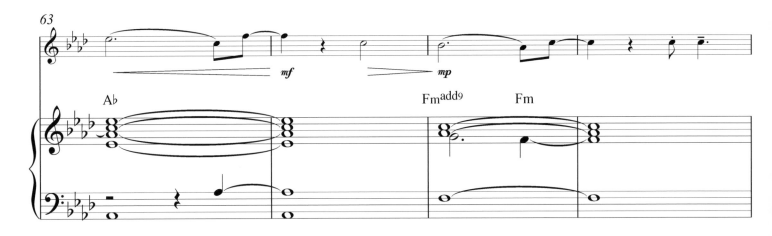

D.S. al Coda

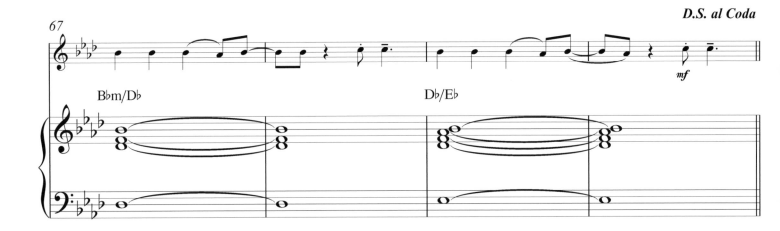

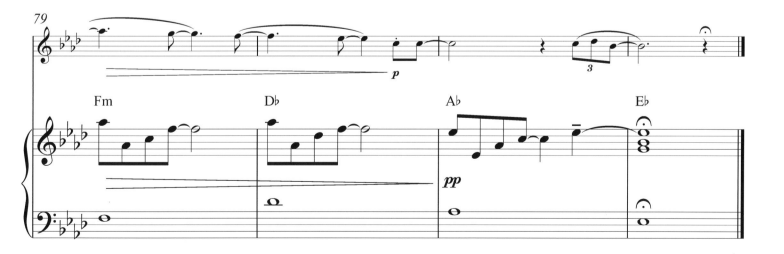

BRIDGE OVER TROUBLED WATER

Words & Music by Paul Simon

Hints & Tips: There are lots of block chords in this piece: make sure you use the correct fingers in anticipation of the next chord position. Watch out for the accidentals too!

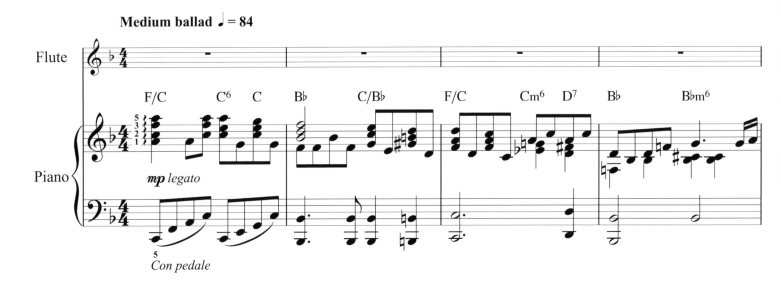

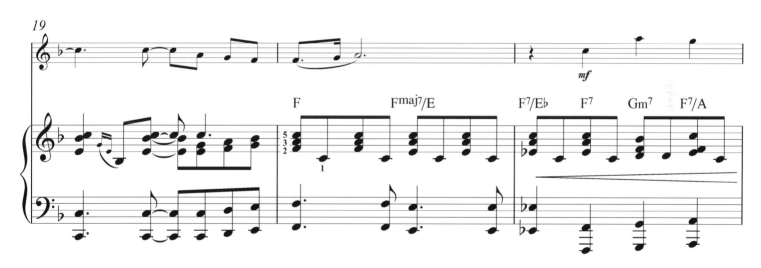

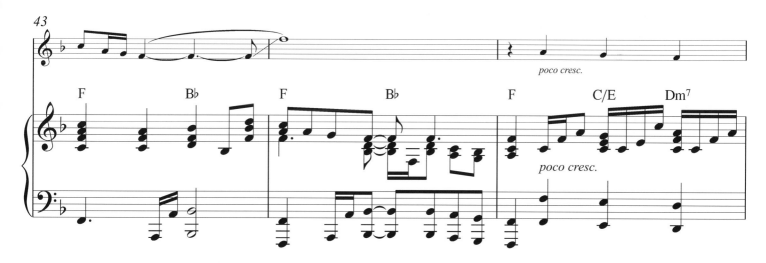

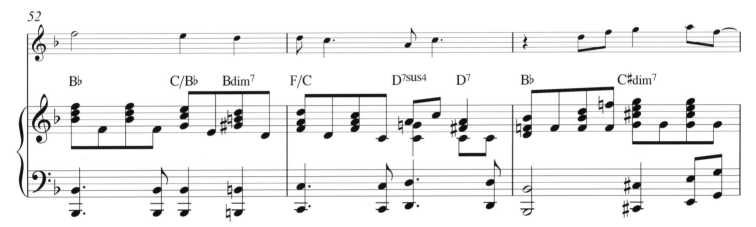

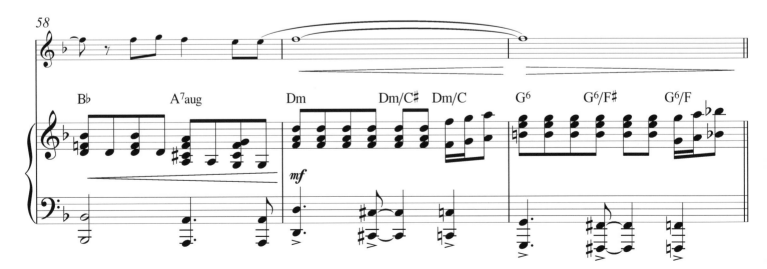

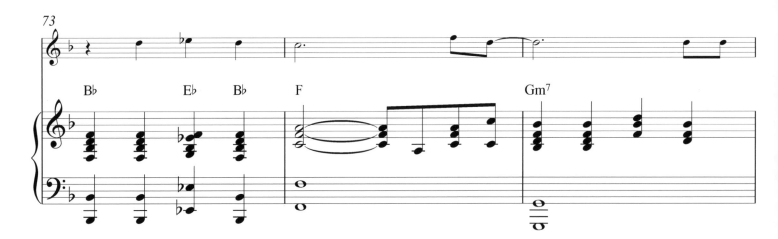

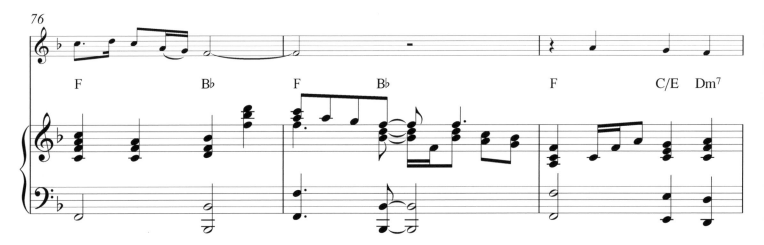

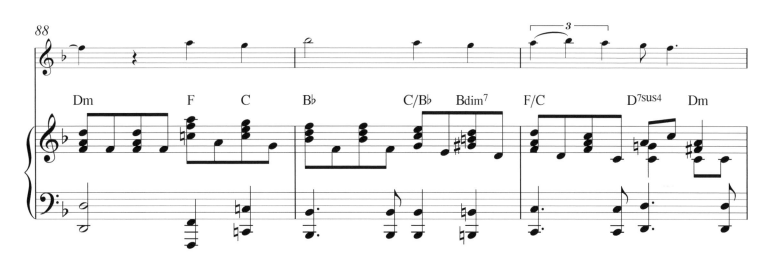

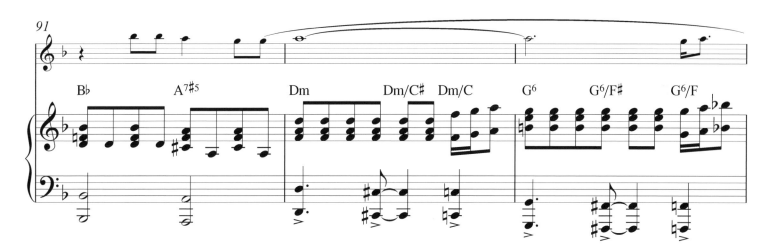

CLOCKS

Words & Music by Guy Berryman, Jonathan Buckland,
William Champion & Christopher Martin

Hints & Tips: Keep the left hand crisp and on the beat and pay attention to keeping a steady pulse. From bar 53 there is a repeated quaver pattern in the right hand played with the 5th finger — make sure the quavers are even as this finger can get tired quite quickly.

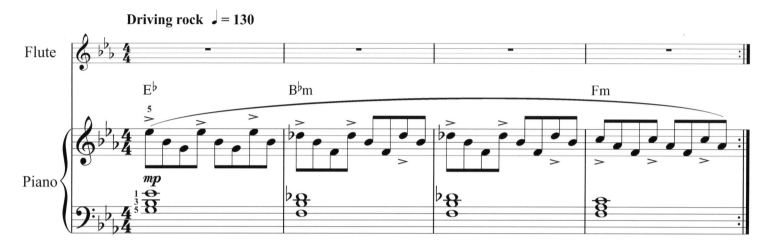

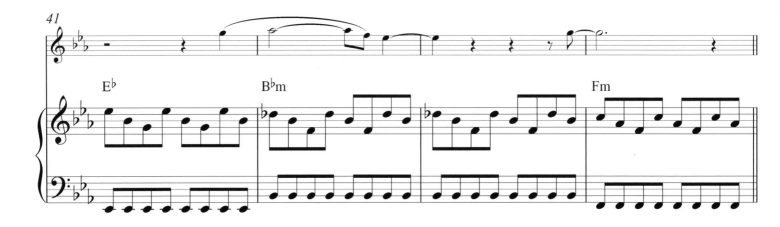

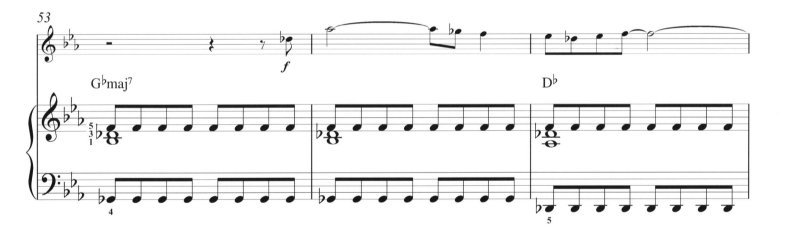

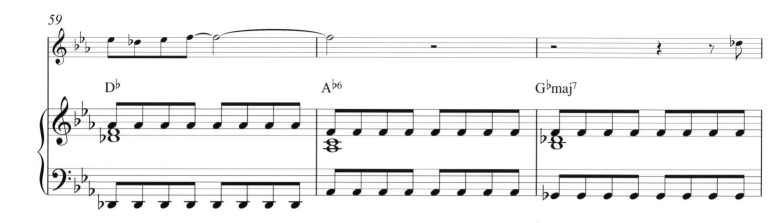

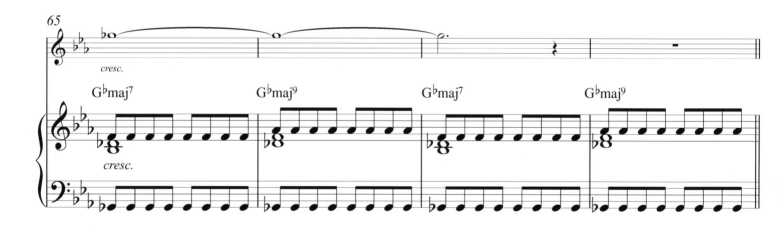

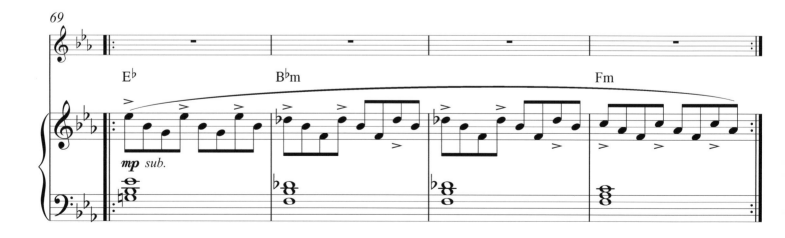

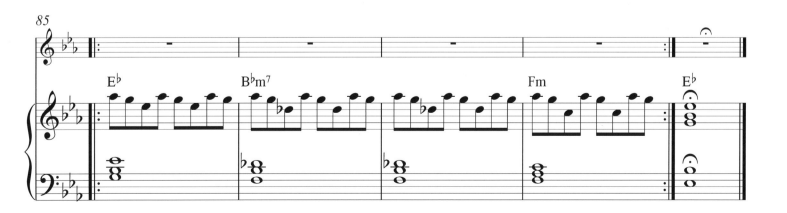

DON'T STOP BELIEVIN'

Words & Music by Steve Perry, Neal Schon & Jonathan Cain

Hints & Tips: Bring out the famous bass line in the left hand and watch out for the off-beat rhythms — make sure you count carefully to ensure every note falls in the right place. Work with the soloist to ensure you play your shared rhythms exactly together in the chorus (e.g. bars 41 and 42).

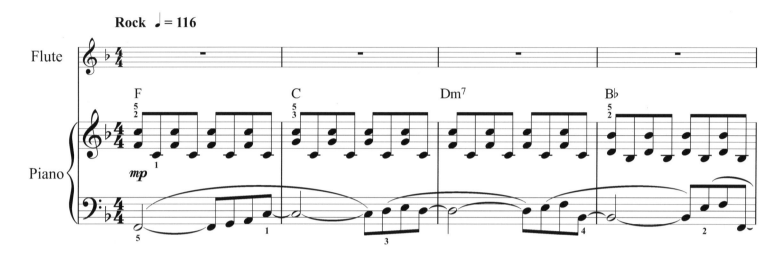

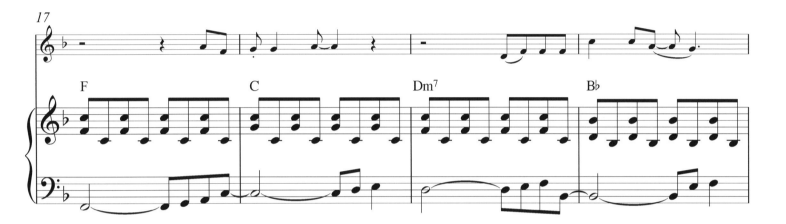

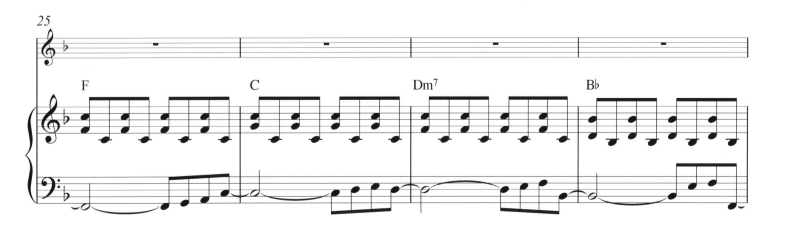

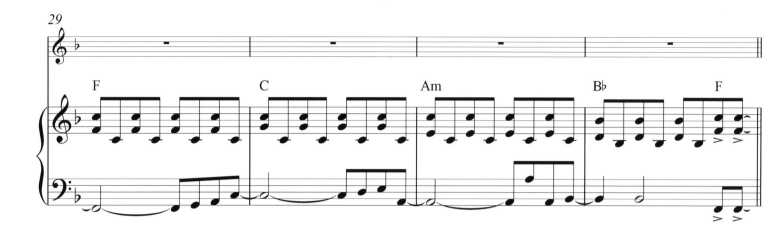

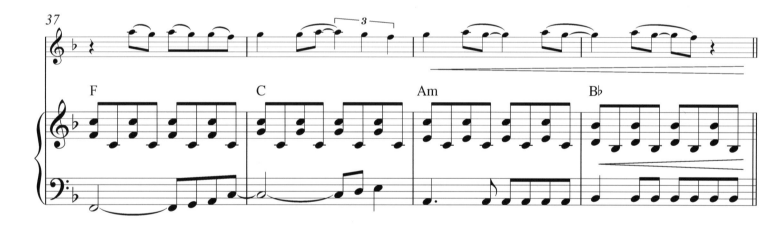

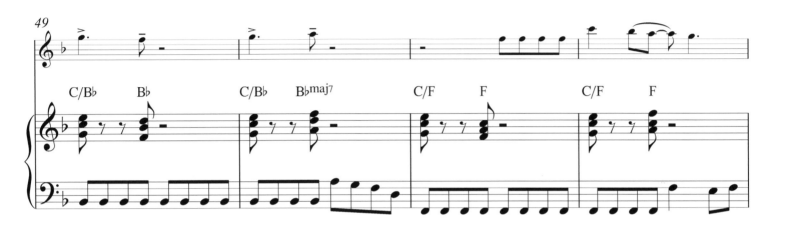

To Coda ⊕

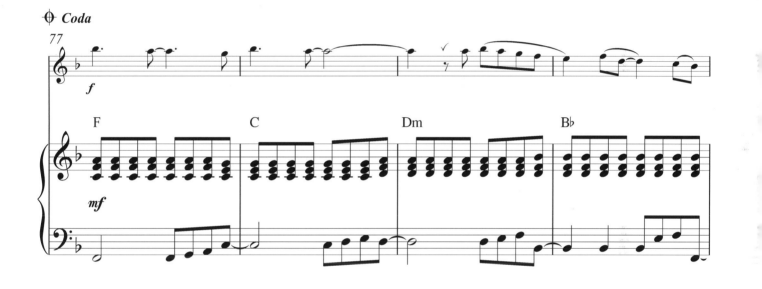

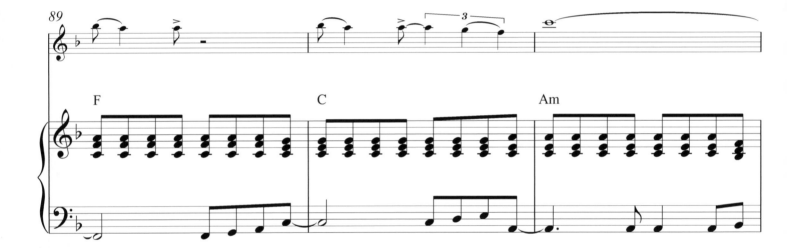

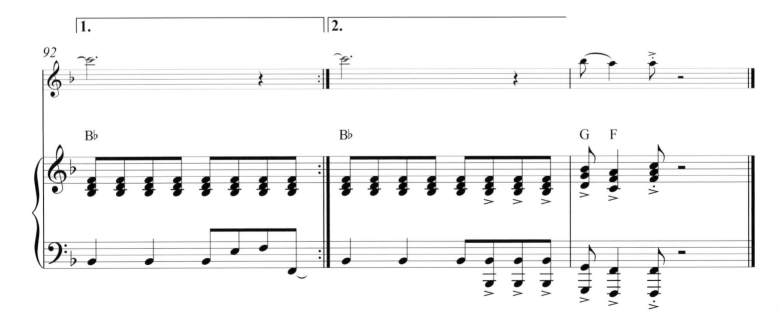

FIREWORK

Words & Music by Tor Erik Hermansen, Katy Perry,
Mikkel S. Eriksen, Sandy Wilhelm & Ester Dean

Hints & Tips: Make sure the driving quaver pattern in crisp and clear throughout.
Watch out for the change to off-beat rhythms at bar 45!

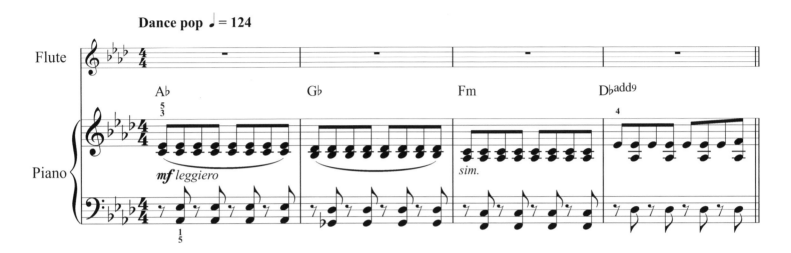

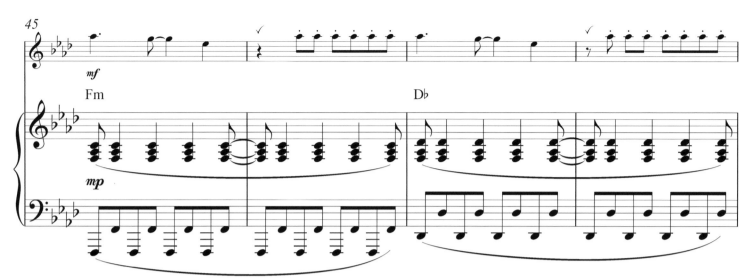

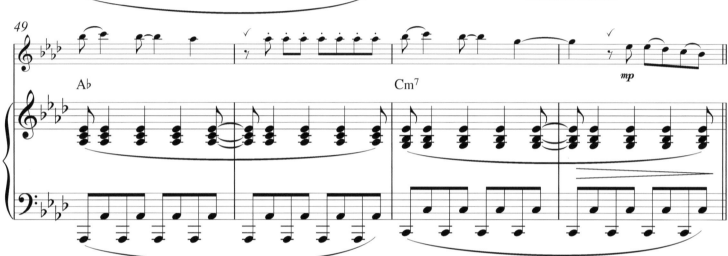

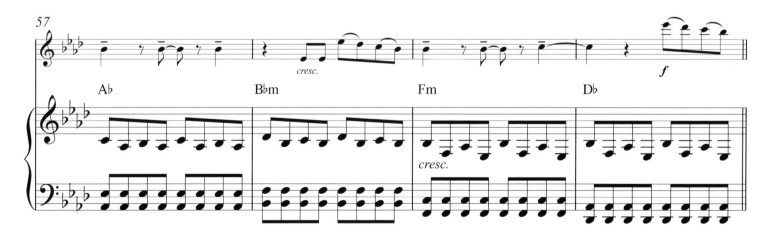

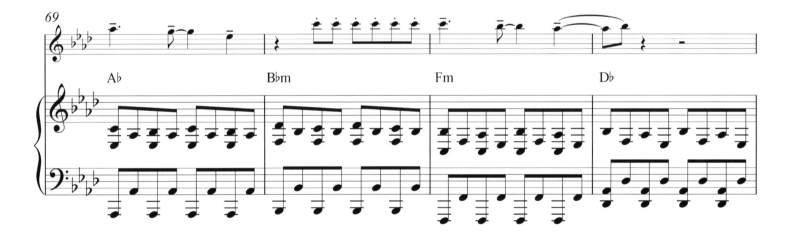

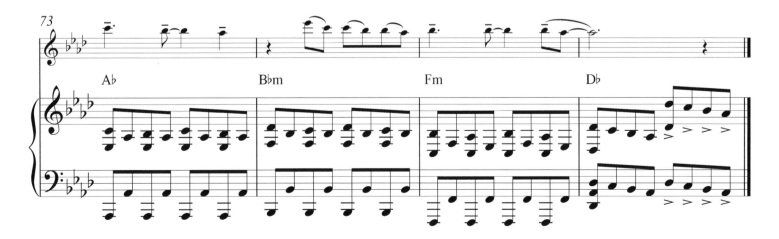

MAD WORLD

Words & Music by Roland Orzabal

Hints & Tips: Make sure the dynamic of the broken chord pattern stays the same when it switches to the right hand in bar 5. Bring out the lovely counter-melody in the right hand at bar 29. The rhythms are less predictable in the right hand from bar 22 — count carefully!

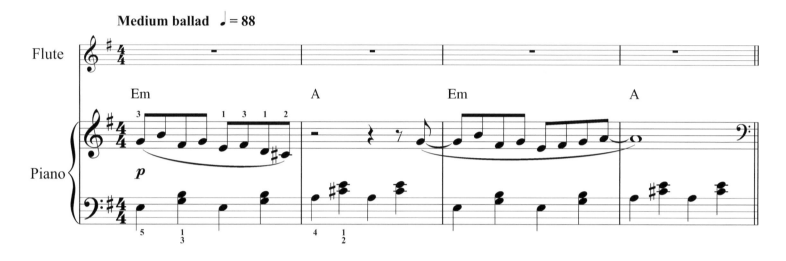

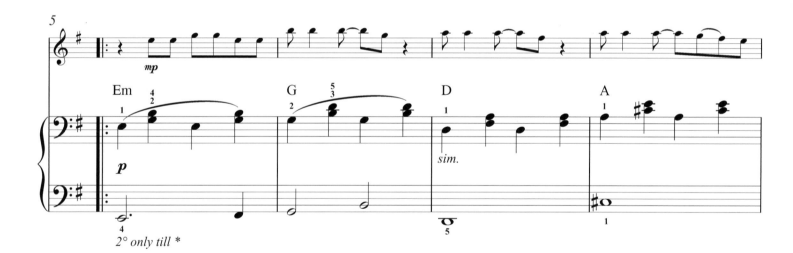

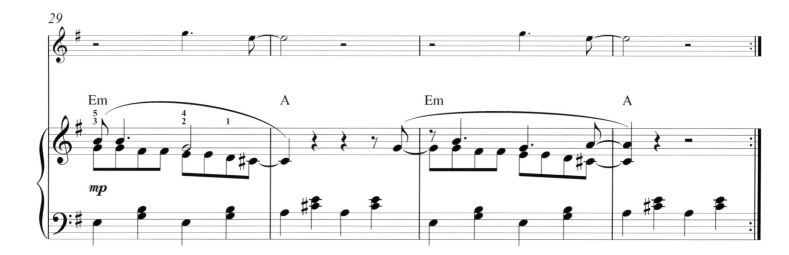

A THOUSAND YEARS

Words & Music by David Hodges & Christina Perri

Hints & Tips: There is a broad range of dynamics in this piece; make sure you make the most of these contrasts. Practise playing the right hand duplets in bar 11 against the quavers in the left hand until you are secure with the rhythms. Use the pedal to sustain the block chords in the right hand from bar 23.

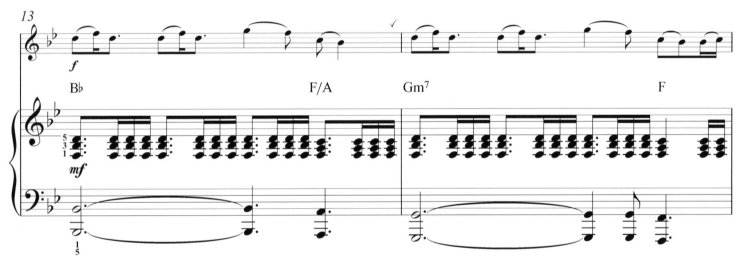

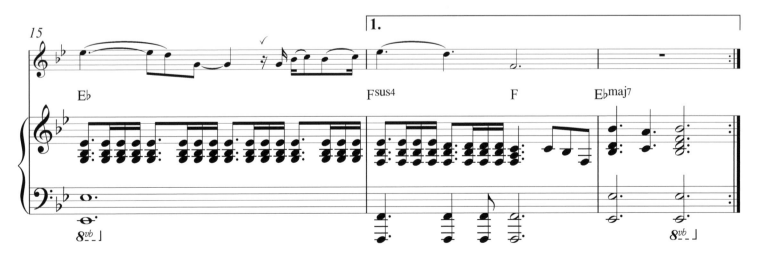

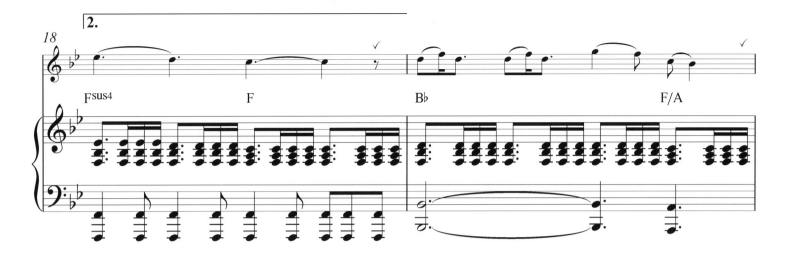

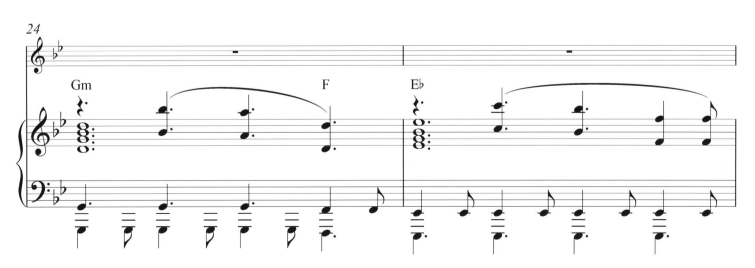

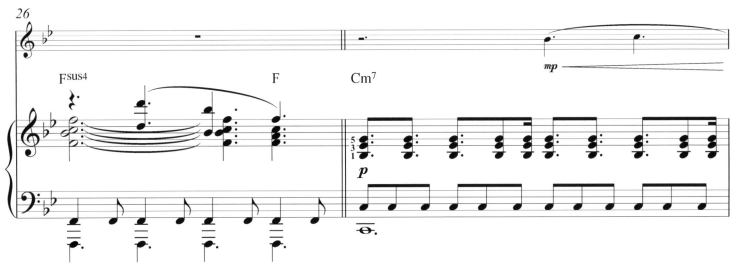

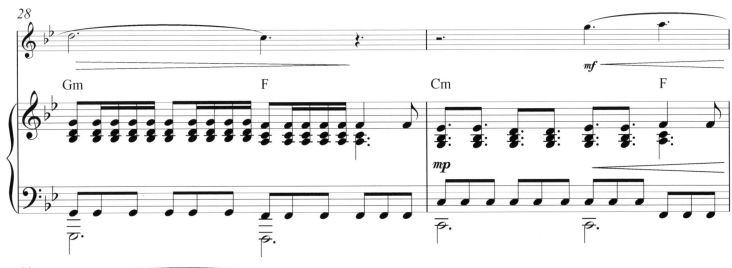

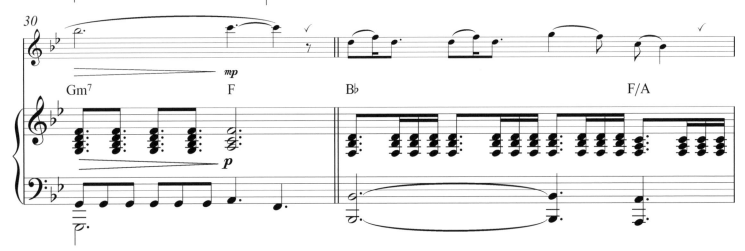

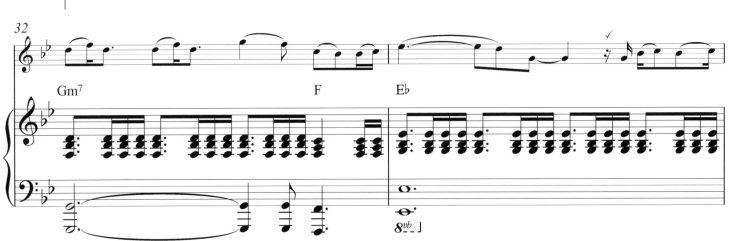

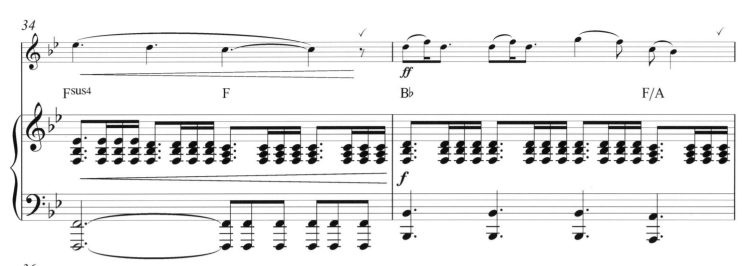

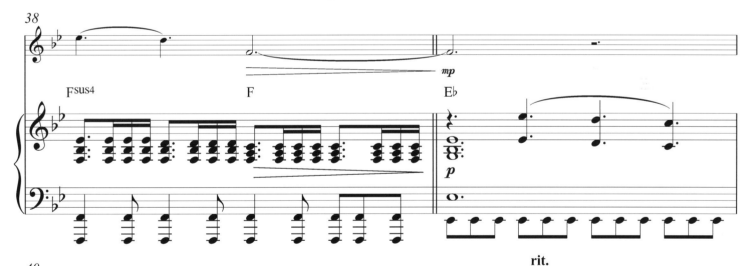

A THOUSAND MILES

Words & Music by Vanessa Carlton

Hints & Tips: This piece features a brilliant piano part! Remember to keep the semiquaver patterns crisp and even. There is a lot of movement in both hands so make sure you're ready for the octave jumps. Practise the call-and-response passages with the soloist (from bars 14 and 40), ensuring you keep to a steady tempo.

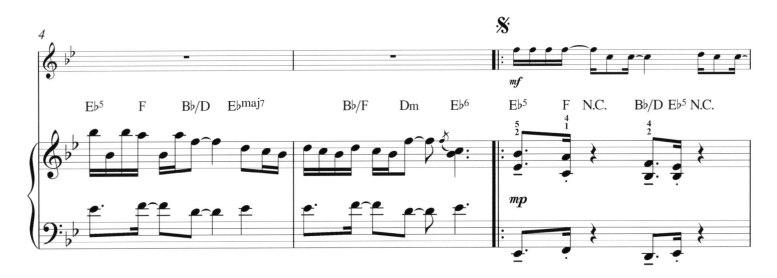

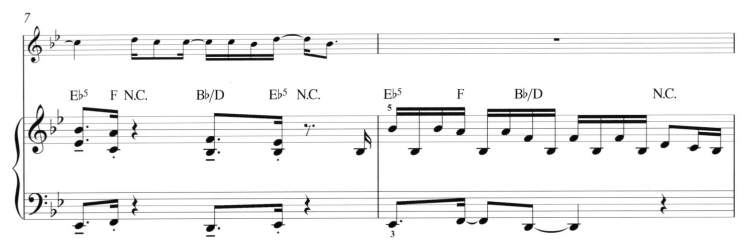

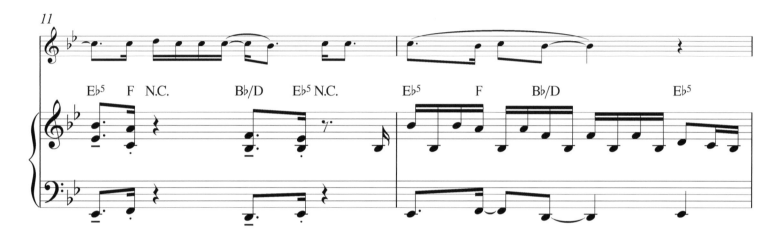

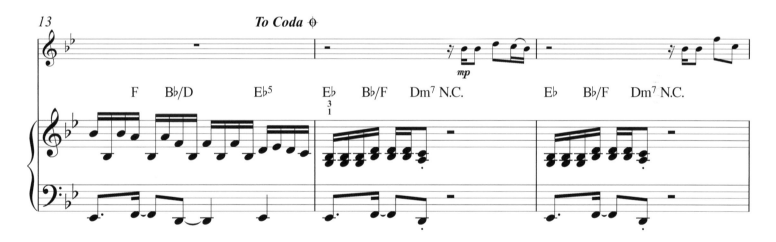

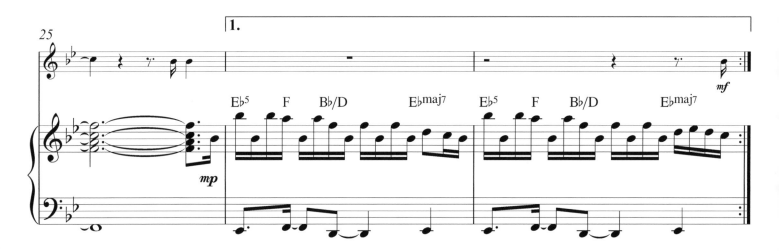

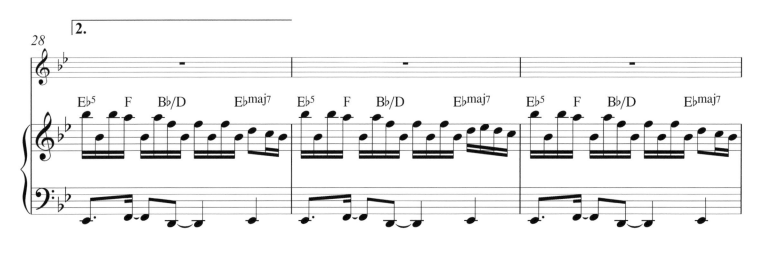

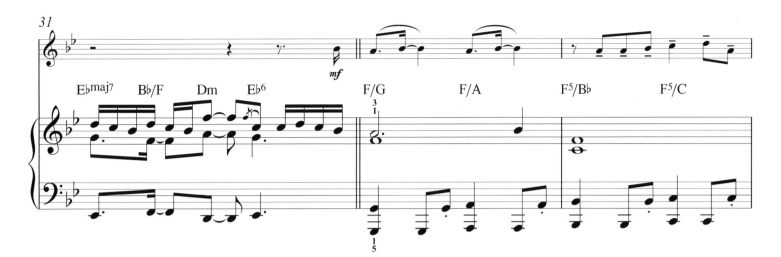

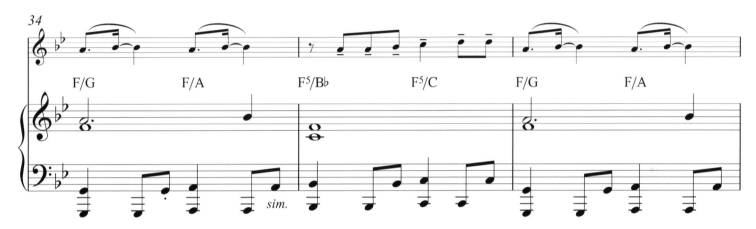

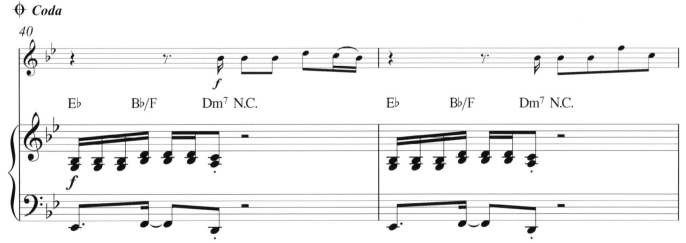

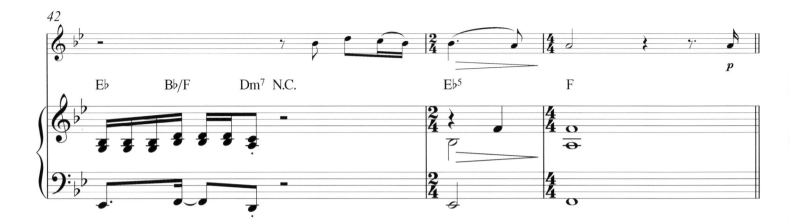

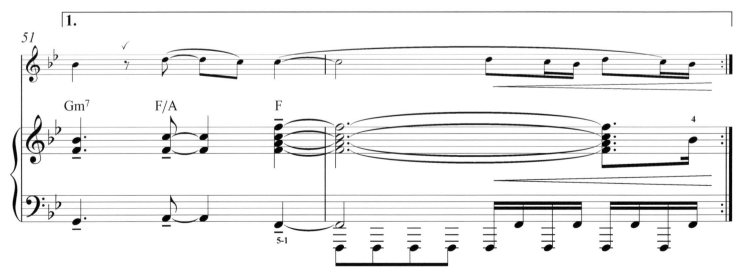

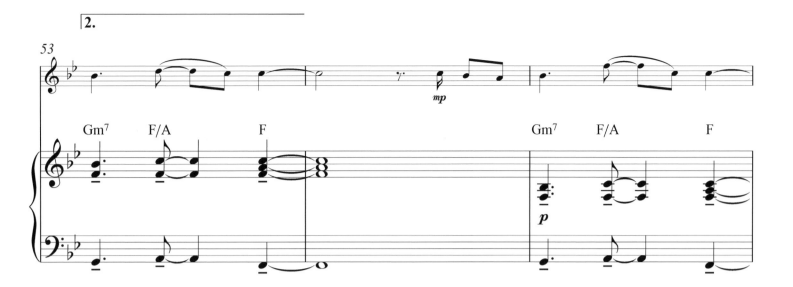

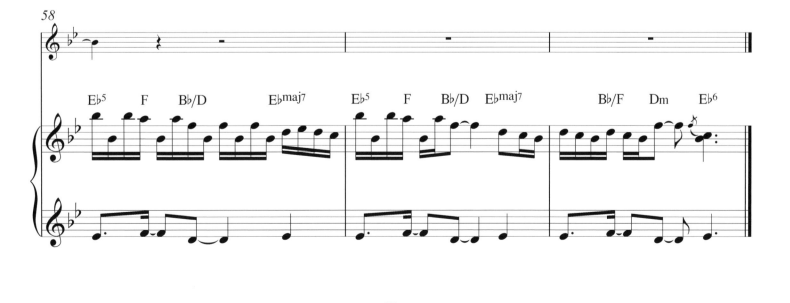

YOUR SONG

Words & Music by Elton John & Bernie Taupin

Hints & Tips: This piano part is quite busy so it's important to be sensitive to the soloist, being careful not to overpower them. Make sure you lift the pedal for every change in harmony so the sound doesn't become muddy. Some of the chords involve big stretches: play all the notes together first to get used to the shapes.

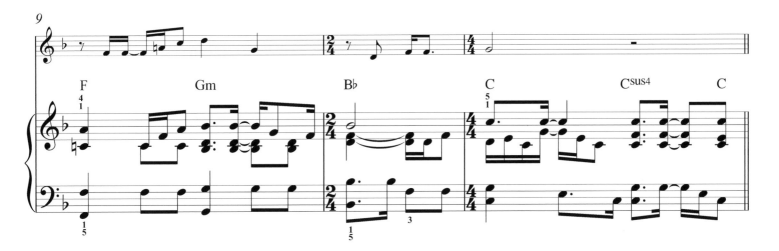

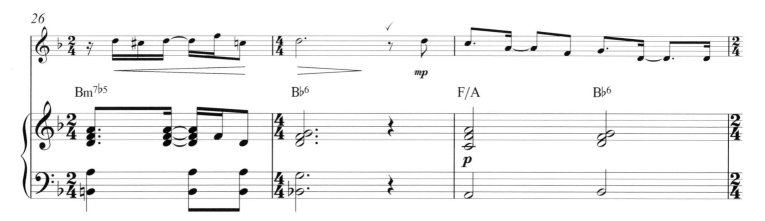

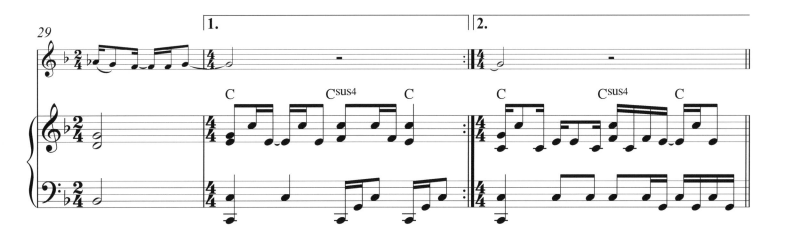

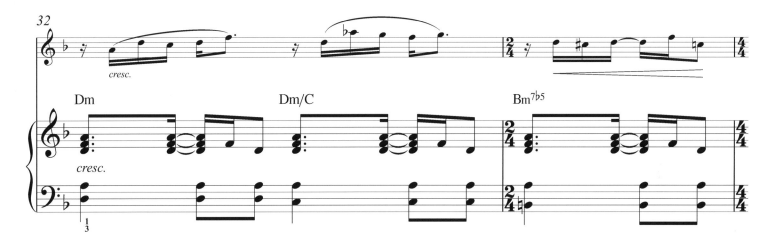

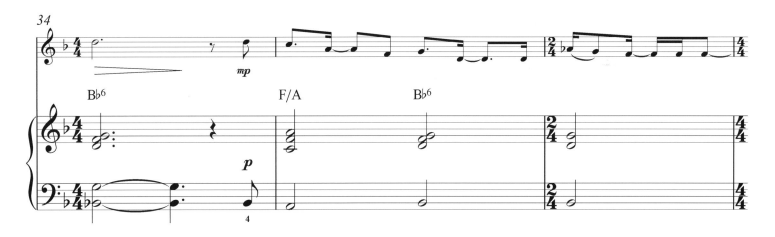

WHEN WE WERE YOUNG

Words & Music by Adele Adkins & Tobias Jesso

Hints & Tips: Work on getting the chord changes as smooth as possible and make sure you feel a steady pulse so you're not tempted to rush the held notes at the start of the piece. If the double octaves in the left hand are too big a stretch, just play the bottom note. Watch out for the big jump in both hands at bar 47!

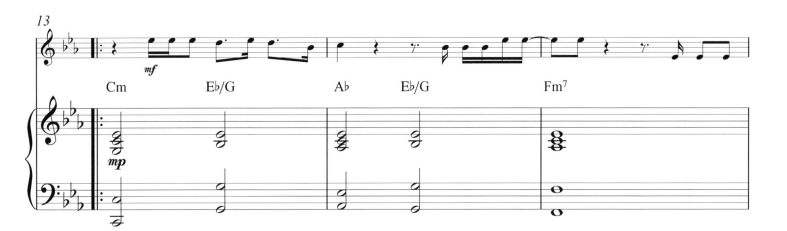

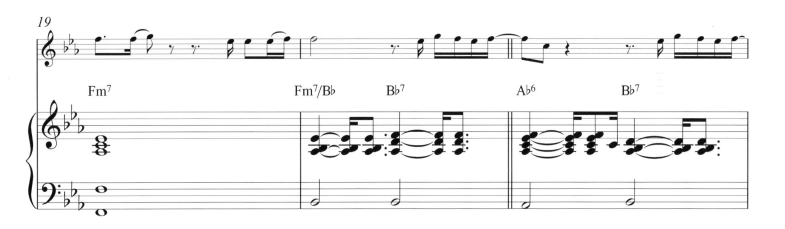

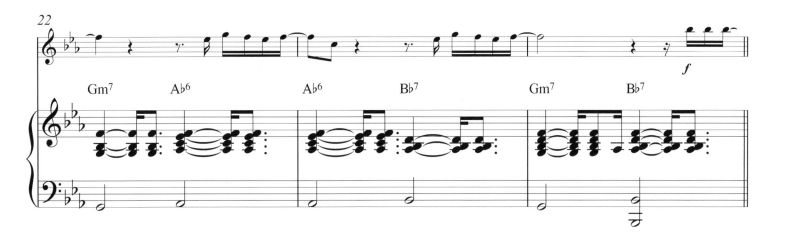

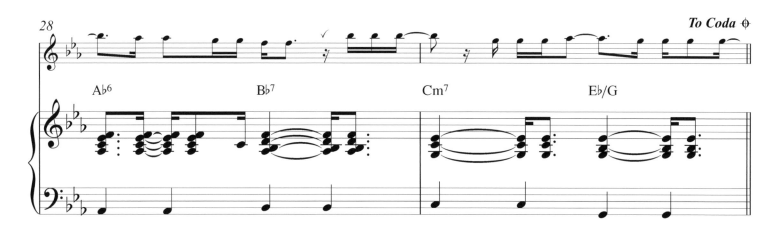

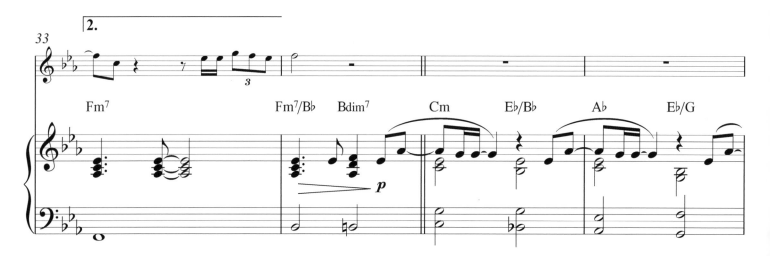

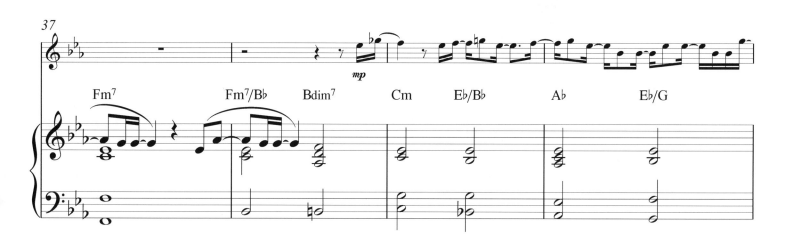

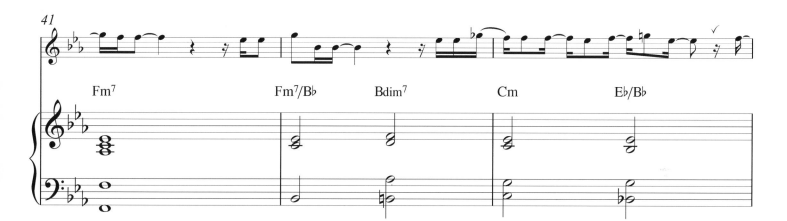

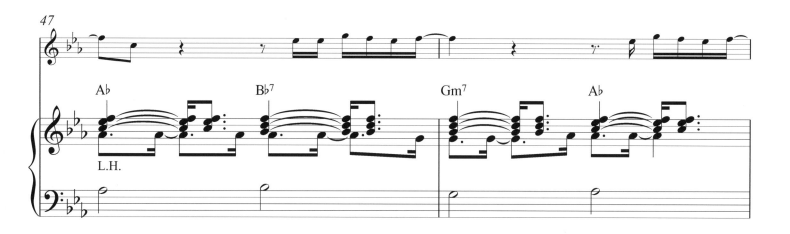

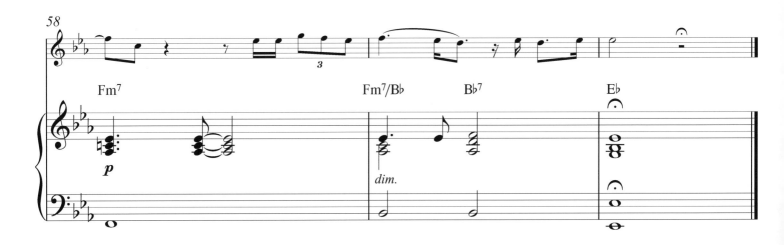

POP PERFORMANCE PIECES

Published by
Chester Music

Exclusive Distributors:
Hal Leonard
7777 West Bluemound Road,
Milwaukee, WI 53213
Email: info@halleonard.com

Hal Leonard Europe Limited
42 Wigmore Street, Marylebone,
London WIU 2 RY
Email: info@halleonardeurope.com

Hal Leonard Australia Pty. Ltd.
4 Lentara Court, Cheltenham,
Victoria 9132, Australia
Email: info@halleonard.com.au

Order No. CH85074
ISBN 978-1-78558-335-3

Piano scores are transposed.
Chord symbols at concert pitch.

Flute consultant: Howard McGill.
Piano consultant: Lisa Cox.
Compiled and edited by Naomi Cook.
Music formatted by Sarah Lofthouse, SEL Music Art Ltd.

Photographs courtesy of Ruth Keating,
assisted by Lisa Cox and James Welland.
Special thanks to the pupils at St Benedict's School, Ealing and
their Director of Music Christopher Eastwood for taking part in
the photo shoot.

Printed in the EU.

www.halleonard.com
www.wisemusicclassical.com

POP PERFORMANCE PIECES

Flute Part

ALL OF ME JOHN LEGEND 4

BRIDGE OVER TROUBLED WATER SIMON & GARFUNKEL 6

CLOCKS COLDPLAY 8

DON'T STOP BELIEVIN' JOURNEY 10

FIREWORK KATY PERRY 12

MAD WORLD MICHAEL ANDREWS FEAT. GARY JULES 22

A THOUSAND MILES VANESSA CARLTON 14

A THOUSAND YEARS CHRISTINA PERRI 16

WHEN WE WERE YOUNG ADELE 18

YOUR SONG ELTON JOHN 20

CHESTER MUSIC
part of The Wise Music Group

ALL OF ME

Words & Music by John Legend & Tobias Gad

Hints & Tips: There are lots of repeated notes in this song; keep them connected with gentle articulation. The middle eight (from bar 54) is syncopated, i.e. played on the 'off-beats'—make sure you stay in time and don't rush!

BRIDGE OVER TROUBLED WATER

Words & Music by Paul Simon

Hints & Tips: The octave glissando from bar 15 to 16 (and 43 to 44) is a tricky one: try to run up an F major scale as quickly as possible and try to 'smear' all the notes together. Also remember to take a big lungful of air at the start of bar 17!

CLOCKS

Words & Music by Guy Berryman, Jonathan Buckland,
William Champion & Christopher Martin

Hints & Tips: This song is an exercise in playing D♭ with a good, solid tone. It's the weakest note on the flute so make sure you support it with diaphragm pressure. Play the chorus (from bar 29) with nice legato phrases.

DON'T STOP BELIEVIN'

Words & Music by Steve Perry, Neal Schon & Jonathan Cain

Hints & Tips: The first verse is set in the low register; try and develop a good, strong sound, especially on the low C in bars 13 and 21. Really let the melody sing out from bar 33, it's in a nice register for the flute.

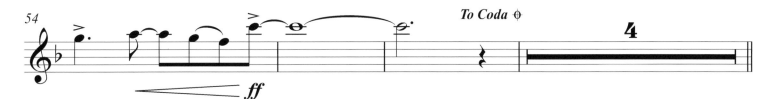

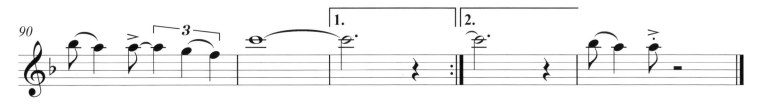

11

FIREWORK

Words & Music by Tor Erik Hermansen, Katy Perry,
Mikkel S. Eriksen, Sandy Wilhelm & Ester Dean

Hints & Tips: This has quite a simple, repetitive melody so it requires you to deliver it in a musical way, building to bar 13. Let the chorus really sing from bar 28! Make sure the tongue is just behind the top teeth making a 'T' sound for the staccato notes in bars 46, 48, 50 and 70.

A THOUSAND MILES

Words & Music by Vanessa Carlton

Hints & Tips: There are some challenging rhythms in this song: keep feeling the semiquaver subdivision all the way through and lock into your very own internal drum machine! You can play the B♭s with the first finger of your right hand using the pad or special key — ask your teacher if you're unsure where this is.

D.S. al Coda

(2° **f**, ad lib. melody)

A THOUSAND YEARS

Words & Music by David Hodges & Christina Perri

Hints & Tips: This piece has a 12/8 groove, i.e. there are 4 beats in a bar with each one sub-divided into a triplet. This all changes in bar 10, when you have to carefully place a 'two against three'. Try to sing this rhythm to yourself before playing the song.

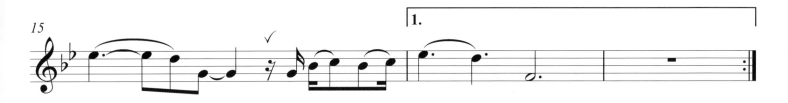

rit.

17

WHEN WE WERE YOUNG

Words & Music by Adele Adkins & Tobias Jesso

Hints & Tips: Remember that you leave off the first finger of your left hand for middle E♭, as you do for D.
Bars 43 and 44 are great for practising syncopated rhythms!

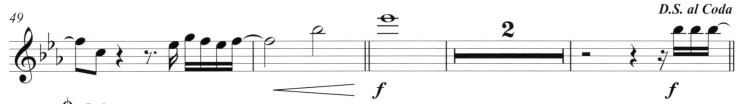

YOUR SONG

Words & Music by Elton John & Bernie Taupin

Hints & Tips: Play the opening of this song with a smooth legato; try not to separate the repeated notes too much. There are lots of 'Scotch snap' (semiquaver-dotted quaver) rhythms—make sure you're ready for them! It may help to clap through the piece first.

mf *joyfully*

cresc.

mp

1.

2.

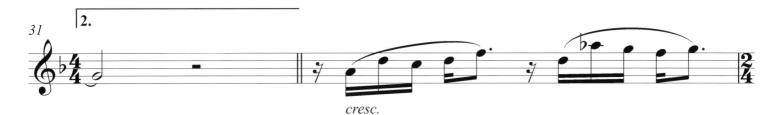

cresc.

mp

MAD WORLD

Words & Music by Roland Orzabal

Hints & Tips: This is a great song for tonguing practice as it has lots of repeated notes.
It's also a good test of rhythmic placement: make sure you don't rush the syncopated notes!

Chester Music
part of The Wise Music Group
CH85074
www.wisemusicclassical.com